ONE GUNNER'S WAR

IN MY GRANDFATHER'S FOOTSTEPS

BARRY WOODHOUSE

ONE GUNNER'S WAR

First published in Great Britain as a softback original in 2019

Copyright © Barry Woodhouse

The moral right of this author has been asserted.

Typeset in Berling

Editing, design, typesetting and publishing by UK Book Publishing
www.ukbookpublishing.com

ISBN: 978-1-912183-84-5

Dedication

*To my **grandfather***

63521 Gunner Reginald Robert Cato.
Royal Garrison Artillery.
101st & 31st Siege Battery.
Killed in Action March 10 1918. Aged 35

also to

57081 Gunner Frank Chapman.
Royal Garrison Artillery.
31st Siege Battery.
Killed in Action March 10 1918. Age unknown

163352 Gunner B. C. Gribble.
Royal Garrison Artillery.
31st Siege Battery.
Killed in Action March 10 1918. Aged 40

*and my **uncle***

123292 Signaller Frederick Basil Woodhouse
Royal Field Artillery
144th Battery
Western Front 1914 - 18
North West Frontier (India) 1919
Died January 1937. Aged 39

For the Fallen

With proud thanksgiving, a mother for her children,
England mourns for her dead across the sea.
Flesh of her flesh they were, spirit of her spirit,
Fallen in the cause of the free.

Solemn the drums thrill: Death august and royal
Sings sorrow up into immortal spheres.
There is music in the midst of desolation
And a glory that shines upon our tears.

They went with songs to the battle, they were young,
Straight of limb, true of eye, steady and aglow.
They were staunch to the end against odds uncounted,
They fell with their faces to the foe.

They shall grow not old, as we that are left grow old:
Age shall not weary them, nor the years condemn.
At the going down of the sun and in the morning
We will remember them.

They mingle not with their laughing comrades again;
They sit no more at familiar tables of home;
They have no lot in our labour of the day-time;
They sleep beyond England's foam.

But where our desires are and our hopes profound,
Felt as a well-spring that is hidden from sight,
To the innermost heart of their own land they are known
As the stars are known to the Night;

As the stars that shall be bright when we are dust,
Moving in marches upon the heavenly plain,
As the stars that are starry in the time of our darkness,
To the end, to the end, they remain.

Robert Laurence Binyon
(1869-1943)

Laurence Binyon composed his best known poem while sitting on the cliff-top looking out to sea from the dramatic scenery of the north Cornish coastline.

The poem was written in the middle of September 1914, a few weeks after the outbreak of the First World War. During these weeks the British Expeditionary Force (BEF) had suffered tremendous casualties following its first encounter with the Imperial German Army at the Battle of Mons on August 23 1914.

Laurence said in 1939 that the four lines of the fourth stanza came to him first. These words of the fourth stanza have become especially familiar and famous, having been adopted by the Royal British Legion as an Exhortation for ceremonies of Remembrance to commemorate fallen Servicemen and women at the Cenotaph in London each November on Remembrance Sunday.

Laurence Binyon was too old to enlist in the military forces but he went to work for the Red Cross as a medical orderly in 1916. He lost several close friends and his brother-in-law in the war. He died in 1943.

Preface

This is my humble tribute to the hundreds of thousands of combatants who lost their lives in the Great War, the War to end all Wars, but especially to my grandfather and two of his comrades who were killed in action on the same day in 1918 and are buried together in the Ypres Reservoir Cemetery, Belgium.

On the 10th of March 2018, I, together with my wife and other family members made a pilgrimage to their graves on the 100th anniversary of their deaths. My wife and I had been several times before to lay a wreath at my grandfather's grave, but this visit was special, not only because it was the 100th anniversary of his death, but because I had been delving into military records, mainly the Commonwealth War Graves Commission records, and I discovered in 2017 that there were two other gunners listed as being killed in action on the same day and with the same siege battery as my grandfather. I can only conclude that they were all comrades in arms and knew each other, fighting alongside each other with the same battery.

What follows is part fact and part fiction. From what information I have been able to gather about my grandfather's movements in Belgium and France with the 101st and 31st Siege Battery of the Royal Garrison Artillery I have recorded here as fact, as are the accounts of battles in which he was engaged in.

This is a story I have woven around these historical facts. All of the service personnel named within were real people who served on the Western Front. The places named are genuine as are all of my grandfather's wartime journey through Belgium and France. The fictional part is however based on fact and I have used my knowledge of the First World War and the Western Front to fill in the many gaps in his story.

Having discovered from various sources some of my grandfather's locations with approximate dates in Belgium and France I have decided to construct around these known facts a story in diary form as he may have recorded. There are many long gaps in dates from the records discovered, so I have only covered the periods known, and as such this book covers the period of March 1916 to September 1917 when the RGA Battery War Diaries and records were destroyed by enemy action and flooding at the battery sites, indeed after September 1917 there are no known surviving records, these were all destroyed by enemy action. I have however very briefly covered a period during early March 1918 when Reginald Robert Cato, Frank Chapman and B. C. Gribble were killed in action. I have also given a Christian name to B. C. Gribble to enable the reader to identify him more readily. My apologies to his descendants for this imposition.

I have faithfully tried to follow the path my grandfather and his comrades took through France and Belgium, but this has proved to be a very difficult task. Recorded place names have been spelt incorrectly and it is quite possible that after the First World War place names were changed - Ypres is now Leper for instance. Another possibility is that some of the smaller towns and villages were so totally destroyed by shellfire that they were never rebuilt, their occupants moving onto other towns to live.

Barry Woodhouse

A brief explanation of Siege Batteries

The 101st and 31st Siege Batteries were just two of the many artillery batteries that were part of the Royal Garrison Artillery (RGA) in Belgium and France during the First World War. There were not only British batteries as Australian, Canadian and South African batteries were formed in Belgium and France from 1916. It would assist the reader to have some knowledge of the history and organisation of the RGA.

The RGA was formed during 1899 as a separate entity of the British Army's Royal Regiment of Artillery (RA) serving alongside the Royal Field Artillery (RFA) and the Royal Horse Artillery (RHA).

A royal warrant dated June 1 1899 effectively separated the regiments of the RA into two corps, the RHA and the RFA becoming one corp, and the RGA the other. Following this the RA was then separated into four other branches, each branch having its own differing shoulder badge to distinguish one from the other - the RGA, RHA, RFA and the RA, the latter being responsible for supplying shells etc. to the other three during times of war.

The RGA was divided into three separate Divisions; the Eastern Division with its headquarters at Dover and depot companies at both Dover and Great Yarmouth; the Southern Division with its headquarters at Portsmouth and depot companies at Gosport and Seaforth, near

Liverpool; the Western Division with its headquarters at Devonport and depot companies at Plymouth and Scarborough.

A siege company was usually commanded by a major together with at least six other lower ranking officers and non commissioned officers (NCOs) - normally 10 NCOs - and up to 200 other ranks. A Siege Battery comprised of four breach loading Howitzer 26 cwt. guns.

It could be said that the RGA were the technical leaders of the RA in so much that during World War 1 they were extremely advanced in technical gunnery - the ability to aim at specific targets rather than saturate enemy positions with shell fire hoping, more by luck than judgement, to hit and destroy the target. These targets could be many miles away from the batteries, but by using map co-ordinates and calculations using geometry and mathematics the targets could be shelled accurately.

Spotter aircraft of the Royal Flying Corp (RFC), supported by forward army observers, passed this information to RGA batteries via wireless telegraphy (Morse code) by the pilot or observer whilst the aircraft was in flight above the enemy lines near the front line, and by land line from the forward land observation posts, and then passed on to the RGA batteries for action.

These batteries were equipped with howitzers that were capable of firing large calibre high explosive shells at a very high trajectory onto enemy positions. The howitzers were referred to by the size of shell they fired - 6 inch, 8 inch, 9.2 inch, and 12 inch, the latter were either road or railway mounted and located some distance behind the front line.

In 1914 the British Army had very few heavy artillery pieces. Very rapidly the RGA became a large part of the army on the Western Front possessing heavy, large calibre howitzers as briefly described below.

The name 'howitzer' describes a cannon (artillery piece) capable of firing a shell in a very high curving trajectory. As an example the British 6 inch, 26-hundredweight (1320 kg) howitzer of World War 1 was developed to outclass artillery used by the German Army. It first entered service with the British Army at the end of 1915. Its specified weight refers to the combined weight of the barrel and its breech.

Prior to 1916 a team of horses would have towed these howitzers, but from 1916 onwards the use of motorised three-ton lorries undertook the role of transportation. To prevent the wooden spoked wheels of the howitzer from sinking into mud or soft earth they were fitted with wooden 'girdles'. Towards late 1917 and into 1918 solid rubber tyres were fitted. Designed by Vickers, all caliber of howitzer - 6 inch, 8 inch, 9.2 inch and 12 inch - were produced by British manufacturers, mainly Armstrong, although one American company also produced howitzers. As the war progressed improvements to the firing capacity and range of shells, the howitzer was improved with many variants.

Shells were defined by size and type of explosive/ammunition they held. Two types of explosive/ammunition were used by field artillery – shrapnel and high explosives. The former was designed to kill infantry. A timed fuse in the shell was set to explode above enemy troops, sending out at high speed and over a large area, shrapnel, best described as metal balls, which would rain down onto troops below. The introduction in 1916 of metal helmets to British troops was to help prevent injury or death if the soldier was caught out in the open and unable to get to cover.

The latter type of shell would contain a high explosive charge fitted with an impact fuse. When striking a hard target such as a building, concrete bunker or hard solid ground, they detonated with incredible force. The blast from these shells and the shell splinters they produced was deadly to unprotected troops. They had one major drawback that when hitting soft, muddy ground, they would not detonate on impact as the fuse would not be triggered to detonate.

The First World War was a highly mechanised war, the first ever in the history of warfare. Artillery tactics were developed through experience. Siege Batteries were developed to destroy enemy artillery positions, strong points such as barbed wire, bunkers and trenches, stores, road and railway systems, and ammunition dumps by firing high trajectory shells onto these targets. A high trajectory meant very destructive firepower as the shell reached high speeds during its decent onto the selected target. Firing at a high trajectory also had the advantage of the shell passing over any obstruction in the line of fire.

The RGA was not only employed on the Western Front. Before war was declared on Tuesday August 4 1914 there were discussions as to the need for air defense over the United Kingdom between the Admiralty and the War Office. The RGA was part of the air defense duties involving some 30 officers and 312 other ranks. The army was given sole responsibility for the air defense of the United Kingdom by February 1916. By May of that year there were 56 Companies of the RGA in existence to operate the guns. In November 1917 the number of personnel had risen to 639 officers and 8,436 other ranks, as well as servicemen of the Royal Engineers and the Army Service Corps.

After hostilities ceased on 11 November 1918 the RGA continued to be an arm of the British Army, but in 1924 the RGA ceased to exist when it was amalgamated into the Royal Artillery from where it originally evolved.

About those who served with the 101st and 31st Siege Battery RGA

63521 Gunner Reginald Robert Cato

Born on 27 December 1885 to Rose Cato (father unknown). From the census of 1891 Rose Cato had married Herbert Crockett and was living at 7 Surrey Place, Tring, Hertfordshire. Reginald Robert Cato (he kept his mother's name of Cato) married Florence May Cook on the 13th May 1908 and lived at 22 Akeman Street, Tring.

Their daughter, Lillian Beatrice Gladys Cato (mother of the author) was born at 6 Henry Street, Tring on 3 June 1913, and on the 11 October 1915 their son, Robert was born.

Reginald was born and bred in the small market town of Tring, Hertfordshire, on the border with neighbouring Buckinghamshire. His schooling would have started, probably from 1889 - 1890, attending Gravelly Infants School just a short distance from where he lived in Akeman Street. Following this he would have then attended the school for junior pupils (mixed) in Tring High Street, before moving 'next door' to Tring Senior School. The author also attended these very same schools some 50 odd years later. (These schools no longer exist sadly. They were all demolished, together with their social history and amazing

Victorian architecture in the 1960s and replaced by a car park and so called 'modern' buildings.)

Receiving only a very basic education Reginald is known to have been employed by a local family owned building company of J. Honour and Sons located near to where he lived. It is believed that he attended the nearby Salvation Army Citadel in Albert Street, directly opposite the cottage in Akeman Street. (The author knows this place of religious worship very well as he attended it.) Although the building still remains it is no longer used as a place of worship, but is now a local community center.

There is no recorded history of his life apart from birth, marriage and death certificates, and of course his service with the RGA, which is very scant. His marriage certificate however does give details of his occupation but little else. I am making a few educated assumptions into his life living in Tring, as, being born in the very same house as he was I obviously know the area extremely well. Even when I was born in 1941 Tring had changed very little if at all, so I grew up in my grandfather's footsteps.

Service with the colours. Reginald was believed to have enlisted on 6 November 1915, serving with the 18th Company Royal Horse & Royal Garrison Artillery until 21 January 1917, first with the 101st and then with the 31st Siege Battery. (This enlistment date is probably incorrect. Conscription started on 2nd March 1916 some months later, and bearing in mind he had just become a father to a baby boy it is unlikely that he would have volunteered. He is first recorded as being on the Western Front from May 20 1916 so could well have been amongst the first to have been conscripted.) His occupation at the time is given as 'builders carter' and was possibly employed in this role by the local family building firm of J. Honour and Sons, based in Akeman Street, Tring.

At sometime during September 1917 he was wounded and suffered the effects of gas and was treated at No. 11 Station Hospital. On discharge he was returned to active service and posted from the 101st Siege Battery to the 31st Siege Battery in the same month.

Killed in action (gassed) at Ypres on Sunday 10 March 1918 aged 35 while still serving with the 31st Siege Battery. He is buried at the Ypres

Reservoir Cemetery, Plot 3, Row C, Grave 25, alongside Gunner B. C. Gribble and Gunner Frank Chapman.

57081 Gunner Frank Chapman.

Before the war he was employed by the Great Western Railway Company as a fireman with the Locomotive and Carriage Department at Abingdon, Berkshire. Just one of the many railway workers who died in World War One.

Killed in action (gassed) at Ypres on Sunday 10 March 1918, age not known, while serving with the 31st Siege Battery. He is buried at the Ypres Reservoir Cemetery, Plot 3, Row C, Grave 26, alongside Gunner Reginald Robert Cato and Gunner B. C. Gribble.

163352 Gunner B. C. Gribble.

He was the son of Mr. and Mrs. G. Gribble, of High Street, Crediton, Devon, and was married to Olive V. Gribble, of High Street, Combe Martin, Devon.

Killed in action (gassed) at Ypres on Sunday 10 March 1918 aged 40 while serving with the 31st Siege Battery. He is buried at the Ypres Reservoir Cemetery, Plot 3, Row C, Grave 24, alongside Gunner Reginald Robert Cato and Gunner Frank Chapman.

An appeal in the North Devon Gazette during 2018 for descendants of Gunner Gribble to contact the author unfortunately proved negative.

Gunner Bennet and Gunner Evens.

These two unknown gunners are also briefly mentioned in the records of the RGA. Sadly there is no further information to identify who they were.

Major-General Harry Lionel Pritchard, CB, CMG, DSO

Born 16 November 1871, Harold Lionel Pritchard was the son of Colonel Hurlock Pritchard and was educated at Charterhouse School.

Commissioned into the Royal Engineers in 1891 he took part in the Fourth Anglo-Ashanti War of 1895. He was then transferred to the Egyptian Army in 1896 and took part in the Siege of Khartoum in 1897, eventually being awarded the Distinguished Service Order (DSO) for service in the Sudan.

He served in the Second Boer War in 1899 and became a Deputy Assistant Director at the War Office in 1904. In 1907 he was appointed Deputy Assistant Quartermaster General in India.

He served in World War I mainly in France and Belgium before being assigned to Egypt where he was Chief Engineer for Middle East Forces in 1916. After the War in 1921, he was appointed as Chief Engineer to the Northern Command and then Assistant Director for Fortifications and Works at the War Office during1923. He held various other engineering positions until his final appointment as Commandant of the Royal School of Military Engineering at Chatham during 1931. Retiring in 1933, he died on 14 May 1953.

Colonel Capp

At Ypres attached to XIX Company Royal Horse Artillery commanded by Brigadier General Pritchard DSO. At the time of publication no further information was available regarding this officer.

Captain R. T. Bolter.

At the time of publication no further information was available regarding this officer.

The Journey Begins
– Arriving on Belgium Soil

1916

Late January

We've completed our basic training where we were taught marching in order and other disciplines the army believes we should all know in an attempt to make us better soldiers. One thing about all of this is that we are a lot fitter and we get fed regularly and very well. The food is quite basic, mainly good old British bangers (sausages) and bully beef; I do believe the British Army marches on bully beef! Some of the lads have put on a lot of weight from when they first arrived here, not a bad thing as some looked very thin and pale, at least the army is feeding us up. For most of us this is our first time away from home and a bit strange. I'm missing Florrie and the children a lot, but the army keeps us so busy doing 'this and that' that there is not too much time to dwell on our home and family.

The NCO drill instructors are a bit fierce, shouting at us all the time, and we always seemed to being doing things wrong, or so it seemed to them. Would you believe that some of the younger lads - our ages range from 17 or so to the late 30s - didn't know their left from their right, causing lots of confusion, and laughs, from us, when we were marching or carrying out rifle drill. I felt sorry for them, but they soon learnt which was which! One of our drill sergeants actually marked in indelible ink the letter 'L' and 'R' onto their hands!

We know what division of the army we are going to so why we have rifle drill and firing practice I'll never know. But if you're in the army then you'll learn about the Lee Enfield .303 rifle, you never know though, we just might have to use it at sometime. I think any German seeing our long bayonet flashing in the sunlight will soon have him running in the other direction!

I've become friendly with two other recruits, Frank Chapman and Basil Gribble. With any luck we should be posted to the same artillery unit after our gunnery training at Lydd, which I think, is in Kent somewhere.

3 February

Artillery training at last. We were all given a weekend pass before coming here to Lydd Artillery Training Camp. Unfortunately not many of us could get home. Transport and time was the problem. None of us want to start our time in the army with a stain on our records as being AWOL - Absent Without Leave - if we got back to camp late. The senior NCOs here are a bit scary, but not as bad as at our previous camp I'm happy to say. They have a job to do so discipline is still pretty rigid, but we do manage a laugh with them on the odd occasion so they are 'human' after all!

We are mainly being taught how to operate a 6-inch howitzer. It's a frightening weapon, particularly if you're not used to noise! We're only firing blanks at the moment, but the tremendous 'crash' they make when firing is deafening. If one or two of us aren't deaf by the end of this war I'll be amazed. Apart from being taught how to work as a team and learning basic howitzer maintenance, we were also expected to dig trenches and gun pits to an accepted standard. This was really hard work, but being very fit from our earlier basic training it didn't prove to be too challenging.

Not content with learning the 'ins and outs' of a 6-inch howitzer we were given instructions on the 8, 9.2 and 12-inch heavies. These are really nasty weapons, capable of firing huge shells high into the atmosphere for many, many miles distance.

Constructing dugouts for ourselves was most challenging though. Do you construct them in the sides of the trenches and gun pits or a distance away from them? We were instructed to dig them a short distance from the pits using the trenches, or saps, as access routes to and from the guns. There's a lot more to this business that just being able to fire a gun!

Sand bag filling was a backbreaking task. One of us would hold the sack open for another to fill with sand or earth from our dug out. The sides are reinforced with corrugated iron sheeting and metal angled stakes, and to make it a bit more 'homely' a corrugated iron roof would go over the top with more sand bags on top of that. As of yet none have collapsed on top of us! Being a gunner is really hard work!

Wrote home to Florrie this evening. Just a short letter telling her and the children that I'm OK and settled into my new enforced life quite well. The billets we're in are all wooden structures and seem to have been erected very quickly, but they are warm - when the two potbelly stoves are alight - and comfortable. Some of the lads do snore a lot however, but a lump of coal thrown in their direction soon stops it! We all have our own wardrobe, well tall cupboard really, to hang our uniforms and other bits of kit.

We still have to endure the dreaded hut and billet inspection. This can be called at any time so we have to make sure every thing is in order and our brass buttons are highly polished. No personal items are allowed, not even photographs of wives, girl friends or family, although I do keep a photograph of Florrie and the children in my wallet.

Nice to see the good old Salvation Army here with a mobile canteen of sorts where we can buy sweet hot tea, a cake or sandwich and newspapers and magazines. Reminds me of home and our Citadel just opposite where we used to live in Akeman Street. I wonder what's happening back home now? There is a chapel, again in a wooden hut, where anybody can go and attend the Sunday morning service. The first attendance is a compulsory Church Parade, after that it's up to us if we want to go or not. I always go unless the army in its wisdom has put me on fire picket or guard duty at our main gate. We all take turns at this, but as we are not allowed off camp it isn't a problem. There's not too much to occupy our minds here in the evening after training and tea. One or two card schools have started up, but no gambling. Any school caught with money on the table and they're for the high jump. The army is very strict about this and the punishment is very severe.

We've been told that once in France or Belgium any conviction for bad behavior, refusing to follow a direct order and so forth is punishable by Number 1 Field Punishment. A very unpleasant punishment as the offending soldier is placed in fetters or handcuffs or some other hand and leg restraint and tied to a gun wheel or fence for anything up to 2 hours each day for any number of days, usually 3 or 4 days of the week for 3 weeks. A bit inhuman in my opinion. I hope I never witness any poor lad being punished like this.

17 March

Today we fired our first 'live' shell on our firing range at quite a high angle. Although it landed some distance away we could feel the earth shake. I would not want to be on the receiving end of one of these! This 'live' firing of shells explains why the camp is so far away from any populated area. The army wouldn't want an errant shell going astray and exploding in some ones back yard!

It's also our last day of training. We've become a well-disciplined team of gunners. Rumor has it that all of the crews are staying together when we get sent to France, which is a good idea. We all know each other well, and operate our gun like a well-oiled machine. Just let us have a chance at getting at Fritz.

Heard from Florrie. Everything is OK at home although the children keep asking her when I'm coming home. With any luck we may get a decent spot of leave before we are sent off. Here's praying.

18 March

I obviously didn't pray hard enough as we were told at parade this morning that we are off to Belgium immediately. This meant lots of packing and preparation. We wouldn't be taking our training guns, they're needed for the next batch of recruits. Our guns should be on their way over as I write this, hopefully we will all meet up in the correct position!

We are going to be part of the 18th Company Royal Horse and Royal Garrison Artillery. Now we really feel as if we are taking part in this war. Look out Fritz, we're on our way!

We marched down to Lydd railway station early this morning after a decent breakfast – more sausages - and collecting our individual rations to last us for two days - the time it would take to get to our new site. We were even given packets of Woodbine cigarettes. The army must believe we'll perform better with a 'fag' hanging out of our mouths!

Travelling by train of the Great Eastern Railway Company, we arrived at Harwich eventually, where on the dockside our boat transport to Belgium was waiting. As it would happen the Great Western Railway Company employed Frank. I don't think he was too impressed with being transported by his competitor!

The army it would seem does everything 'by numbers'. Marching to the station was in columns of four, left, right, left, right; shoulder dressing by numbers etc., etc. Embarkation onto the ship was again 'by numbers'. "In columns of two, forward march!" Just like basic training again! This time up the gangplank in lines two abreast, but it works. All nice and orderly, although we abandoned keeping in step much to the annoyance of the NCOs.

20 March.

We arrived by boat from Harwich in the early hours of the morning with the rest of the lads from the 18th Company, RH and RGA. It was quite a calm crossing thankfully, and only a few of us were sea sick, not too many of us managed to get any sleep, we were like schoolboys on holiday, just too excited at what was in front of us.

None of us are quite sure what to expect now we are on Belgium soil at Zeebrugge, at least, I think that's where we are, but knowing the army we could be at Dunkirk which is in France or any other place for that matter.

We learned on the way over that Fred was a fireman with the Locomotive and Carriage Department at Abingdon. A bit of a joker who keeps us all amused with tales from his railway days. One of his first jobs after firing up the steam engine was to cook breakfast on a shovel put into the firebox. He reckons that egg and bacon tastes a lot better with some good old coal smoke and dust to add flavour to it!

As for young Basil, well he's the quiet type, the exact opposite of Frank, but a good chap just the same. Some of the other gunners have a nickname for him - Bashful Basil. I don't think Basil knows about this, but being good hearted I'm sure he won't take offense by it. He's probably a bit on the shy side because this is the first time he has ever left his home in Devon, but for that matter it's the first time for most of us What an adventure we're going to have. They reckon it will all be over by Christmas so I hope we have a chance at kicking Fritz up the backside! Basil lives in a town called Combe Martin where his mother and father live together with his new young wife Olive. I feel really sorry for him in a way, just married and he's dragged off to war not knowing when he will see his young wife again.

I'm not sure if I should really keep a diary, well it's a record really, of where we go and what we do, but I promised my wife Florrie that I would write down as much as I could. If I get caught I know I'm in deep trouble as it's strictly against Army orders to do this. I don't fancy being caught and getting Number 1 Field Punishment. The other lads know, but I can trust them not to say anything. I miss my daughter Lily and my newly born son Robert, but hopefully we shall all be given leave at some time and hopefully get back to Blighty to see them all again.

Field Punishment Number 1 really was an inhuman form of punishment inflicted on British soldiers during World War 1. Introduced in 1881 it replaced the flogging of offending soldiers. Commanding Officers could award Field Punishments for up to 28 days, whereas a Court Martial offence could be awarded for up to 90 days.

The punishment consisted of the guilty soldier either being attached by handcuff or something similar, to a fence post or wagon wheel for two hours each day, but not for every day of his punishment period. Often nicknamed by soldiers as a 'crucifixion' as the arms would be stretched out and the legs tied together. Some 60,210 such punishments were carried out during World War 1.

These punishments usually took place behind the lines in field punishment camps. There are conflicting stories that when the soldier's unit moved to the front line his punishment continued nearer to the trenches within range of enemy fire, but I could find no record of this ever happening - but that doesn't mean it didn't.

20 May

This is the first time I've had to make some notes in my diary. I haven't been able to write home, so I hope Florrie isn't getting worried about no news coming from me, but what do they say - no news is good news - I hope that's right!

Since arriving on the Western Front at Edelion or some such name, we have been busy with more training and instruction on operating a siege howitzer as part of the 101st Siege Battery. Ours is a huge 8-inch howitzer that really packs a punch and can do a lot of damage to the German trenches and anything else we are ordered to attack. I certainly wouldn't want to be on the receiving end of one of our shells!

The weather is really atrocious. Rain, rain and still more rain. I thought England could be wet but Belgium is definitely the wettest place I have known, not that I've travelled a lot! The conditions in the front line trenches must be particularly nasty. Our lads having to contend with not only enemy snipers taking a pot shot at every opportunity but mud as well. How they manage to keep dry is beyond me, but then, perhaps they don't and just put up with it. At least they get moved back behind the lines to rest areas to get cleaned up and rested while another unit takes their place, a sort of a rota system.

We have heard rumours that we will be on the move soon closer to our front line, so we could be in action at long last. All of this daily training is fine but it will be good to put it to some good use. Frank, Basil and myself often talk about what we can expect nearer the front. We will be positioned a few miles behind the line so won't witness the effect of our barrage on the Hun which is a pity, but we intend to give him a bloody nose all the same!

We will probably have to prepare new positions, as we will be more than likely taking our own guns with us rather than relieving another battery. More digging and sand bag filling! Oh well, never mind. At least we can construct the site to our own satisfaction rather than taking over from another batteries attempt!

I managed at long last to send Florrie a postcard today. Couldn't really write a lot, just to say I was safe and sound and missing her and the children a great deal especially little Robert and for the most part I was keeping busy. Our cards are censored so we have to be careful what we write. I'm not too happy about somebody else reading it before Florrie does but that's the way it has to be, just in case somebody does write something down which might be helpful to old Fritz, although the chances of him getting hold of any mail is a bit unlikely, but you never know. Better to be safe than sorry.

14 June

Those rumours were right. I'm not sure how the word manages to get around, but get around it does! There was a meeting of all the Battery Commanders this morning so we all knew something was afoot. Next the commanders are calling all the senior NCOs together, no doubt to pass on orders and instructions which they would then give to us gunners.

There's a good chance we're moving into France to support our own BEF *(British Expeditionary Force)* and the French Army on the Somme River. It looks as if there is going to be a big push against the German Army entrenched on the river and we are going to shell and destroy their barbed wire, trench systems and strong points. A bit of action at long last. All the lads are very keen to have a good go at the Hun. This will be our first time in action so I hope we perform well and put all those months of training and firing practice into some good use. Our officers and NCOs are really top class, and like us are keen to get into action. Some have seen action already and they are giving us new lads lots of advice, encouragement and confidence in what is to come over the next few days or weeks.

The orders to hitch our guns to horse drawn transportation was given this afternoon. I've never seen so much activity. Horses and men, plus guns of course, seem to be all over the place. It looks like total chaos but each and every man knows his job and everything is ready for our move later this afternoon. Once everything is prepared we have a quick meal, good old bully beef again! We've been told we're heading for a town in France called Albert, not too sure where abouts that is as only the officers have maps of any kind. No doubt we will find out more once we arrive there. Watch out Hun, the 101st Siege Battery is on its way!

21 June

Everything has been a bit hectic this last week so I haven't been able to keep my diary up to date. We've taken up new positions a few miles from Albert, I can't tell you where exactly as that is a secret, so to write it in my diary will get me into a lot of trouble if I'm found out! We're settled in here with some good deep dugouts where we can rest up, eat our meals delivered each day from the rear and generally keep ourselves clean and tidy which at times is just about impossible, but we all do our best.

The service lads are bringing up thousands of shells from depots at the rear. I didn't realise it but the engineers have laid a narrow track railway line to get the shells from the depots as quickly as possible. Frank was pretty impressed to hear this being an ex railway worker. I think he's hoping to go to the rear to take a look, but I very much doubt if that will happen.

We prepare our shells for firing, taking them out of the metal canisters they arrived in, these will be taken back to the rear for further use, the shells being stockpiled near to our gun ready for action.

24 June

Everything is happening very quickly now. We are to start bombarding the German trenches and wire in preparation for the French and British infantry to attack the south bank from a town called Foucaucourt to the Somme and north to Gommecourt. Rumour has it the infantry belong to the French Sixth Army and the good old British Fourth Army. We all mean to give the German's a bloody nose and to give our boys the best possible chance when attacking.

This is when months of training really show. Frank, Basil and myself are responsible for preparing the shells, loading them in the breech and the firing. It all works0 like clockwork, every action and movement happens as if we are in the same, repeating dream. We trust each other without question to get each part of the sequence correct. The rest of the gun crew have their own duties to keep our gun in action; supplying Fred with shells from our storage area to aligning our gun to keep the trajectory as it should be, a very important role that, as if our trajectory is wrong the shells won't hit their designated target.

The noise from thousands of guns that start firing simultaneously along our front is deafening. We maintain a steady rate of fire, only stopping temporary when ordered to by our battery NCO who is receiving orders from our headquarters in the rear by field telephone. Fritz is bound to spot our firing positions so at some time we can expect return fire on our positions from his heavy guns, unless of course they keep their heads down while our heavy guns fire on his positions.

Firing up to ten shells each minute is pretty hard work, and although we are stripped to the waist we are all drenched in sweat. The continual bending down, loading the shell in the breech, firing and then discarding the shell casing to behind our gun where another of our crew remove it for later collection all takes a lot of energy. We work in complete silence, not that we would be able to hear each other above the noise of the battery guns anyhow. Each man knows what to do and when.

28 June

We've been in constant action for five days now. When will it stop? Surely there cannot be much more of the German's trench and barbed wire system left intact. Although the Germans are our enemy I really do feel for the young soldiers trying to shelter from our barrage. It must be absolutely terrifying. Best not to think too much about that as our lads will soon have to go 'over the top' to face them. God bless them all and look after them as they cross no-man's-land.

More shells are delivered to our batteries, thousands of them. If Fritz puts one of his shells amongst this little lot you'll hear the explosion in Blighty. Fortunately we're well camouflaged in a large wooded area to hide us from German spotter aircraft that seem to be looking for us. More than once we've seen our own aircraft chase after them, but as yet haven't seen any German aircraft shot down. The Germans zoom off pretty quick as soon as our 'planes appear. If Fritz doesn't know something's afoot with this continual shelling then he really doesn't deserve to win this war, not that he will anyway!

We all spotted something very new and frightening this afternoon, tanks, dozens of them, have just arrived, all well hidden under the trees near where we are. I wouldn't want to have to face one of these iron monsters at the front, they really are terrifying machines. Some have machine guns while others have artillery pieces jutting out from the sides. They don't have wheels but iron tracks on each side to move them across the ground. Most have been given names. I spotted 'Deborah' and 'Fray Bentos' – what a surprise - earlier on. The crews refer to them as 'male' or female' tanks depending on what armaments they carry. None of us are sure which is which. We're going to try and get a closer look at them later on and meet the lads that operate them when we get a break from firing.

'Fray Bentos' was, and still is, a well-known brand of bully beef!

I July

Eventually we were given the order to cease-fire. Being behind the front lines there is no way of us gunners knowing what is happening at the front, but we all suspect that our boys are preparing to 'go over the top' and attack the German lines. May God look after them all. I cannot begin to imagine what our lads must be thinking waiting in their trenches for the officer to give the order to attack. We've been told that each Tommy is given a tot of rum before the attack to help calm any nerves, I think I would need several tots to keep calm!

The Battle of Albert lasted until 13 July, covering the first two weeks of the Battle of the Somme offensive by British and French infantry. The French Sixth Army together with sections of the British Fourth Army inflicted a massive defeat on the opposing German Second Army. The British attack from the Albert - Bapaume road to Gommecourt however was a complete disaster that cost the British Army some 60,000 casualties in total, most being inflicted during this attack by the German defenders.

After a week of very heavy, continuous rain, the British divisions located at Picardy began the attack supported by five French divisions to their right. Seven days of heavy shelling on the German defenders preceded the offensive, but had failed to destroy barbed wire defences or the trenches. The British Army on this single day suffered the highest casualties ever in a single day, in the region of 57,000 men, killed, wounded or missing.

Against French Marshall Joseph Joffre's wishes, British General Sir Douglas Haig abandoned the offensive north of the road in an attempt to reinforce the successes gained in the south. It was here that British and French forces pushed forward to the German's second line of defence in preparation for a second attack on 14 July.

The Battle of Bazentin Ridge lasted for four days in which the British Fourth Army attacked the German second line of defences from the Somme near Guillemont and Ginchy, along the crest of a ridge to Pozieres located on the Albert to Bapaume road.

There were three villages to be attacked and captured - Bazentin le Petit, Bazentin le Grand and Longueval. Commencing at 03.35 following a short artillery bombardment, the infantry attacked into no-mans-land under cover of a rolling barrage fired a few hundred yards in front of them, aimed to keep the German defenders under cover while the troops advanced. Once the barrage lifted from the German front trenches the troops had a short distance to reach these trenches and attack the defending German troops.

Most of the objectives were secured, but the gains achieved were not taken advantage of mainly because of British communication failures, heavy casualties which were not replaced, and disorganisation caused primarily by failures in communication from the front to rear echelons.

The final battle during what is referred to as the First Phase of the Battle of the Somme was the Battle of Fromelies, 19 and 20 July. This is where Australian forces were first involved in action. Described today as the worst 24 hours in Australian Military history. Over 5,500 Australian troops became casualties in one day during the attack by the 5th Australian Division.

Intended to support the British Fourth Army on the Somme some 50 miles (80 kilometers) to the south, the attacking Australian troops lacked experience in trench warfare, plus the strength of the defending force was drastically underestimated. The Germans had a 2:1 superiority in numbers. The battle gained no ground and German losses were no more than 2,000 compared to a total of over 7,000 Allied casualties.

16 July

A rapid move to a new location. We were rushed to a town called Longueval. None of us are really sure where abouts in France we are. We just get ordered to hitch up our gun and equipment to be transported to our new site. Only the officers have maps so we just get on with it. All we did know is that we were to give support to our lads on the right flank of the BEF who were to attack a place called Delville Wood while another attack takes place to capture higher ground at High Wood and Pozieres.

From what we were told the aim was to capture several fortified villages and woods that were well defended by German troops. High points that offered observation positions for our artillery fire were also objectives together with any other tactical advantages. I must say that our officers and NCOs always pass on information to us so that we know what we are doing and why.

As it turned out our batteries were not used for some reason, so some disappointment all round. News filtering back from the attack led us to believe that it had been successful although casualties were high. We all hope it was worth the sacrifice.

16 September

We stayed here at Longueval until the middle of September. In that time we took no further part in firing our guns in anger. This unexpected break gave us all time to maintain and repair our howitzers to bring them up to top line condition. We also took the opportunity to clean ourselves up. Although KR *(King's Regulations)* required men of all ranks to have a moustache most of us arrived in Belgium and France clean-shaven, but we now all supported a moustache! Some were quite neat and tidy, but the majority were of the 'shaggy dog' appearance! God knows what my Florrie would think if she could see me now. I suspect she would tell me to shave the offending facial hair off before I could kiss her and our two children.

This welcome break from action also gave us the chance to get cleaned up. We hadn't washed properly or been able to change our clothes for weeks now. Most of us had lice to some degree and this was the opportunity to rid ourselves of our little unwelcome visitors. Empty drums of every description were quickly filled with boiling water and disinfectant into which our underwear, shirts and socks were washed. Once they were given a thorough beating and scrubbing we hung them out to dry, hopefully minus our little friends! We did hear that we were to be issued with new clothing, but as yet this hasn't happened. I pray that it wasn't a rumour as conditions here, although not too bad, could do with some improving, but we just get on with it and do the best we can. What conditions are like at the front doesn't bear thinking about. We've heard stories of huge rats feasting on the corpses of soldiers that are not buried. No way for a brave soldier to go!

Blank postcards were issued to us while we were here to write home, only our second opportunity to do this since we arrived. We could only really say how we were fairing, any mention of where we were or what we had done was strictly forbidden by the census people. Florrie must be worried by the lack of news from me, but I think she'll understand how difficult it can be to keep in touch. Who knows, I might even get a letter back from her, if she knew where to send it! All she could really do is to address it to me care of the BEF somewhere in France. Slim chance of it ever reaching me but I can pray that it will.

We all had some well-earned leave last weekend. We were allowed to travel to some little French town, the name of which I cannot remember. It seems years ago since we walked along proper pavements and met 'ordinary' people. Looking in shop windows at some of the goods on sale was an experience for the three of us, Basil, Fred and me, as we wandered from shop to shop seeing what was on offer.

Coming across a pub, the French call them bars, we decided to treat ourselves to some French beer, lager they call it. Different we all agreed. Give us a proper pint of real British ale any day of the week, but beggars can't be choosers as they say! We had a bit of a contest between us while supping our 'lager' – who had the most pubs in their home town! I estimated there are at least seven or eight public houses spread about Tring. I attempted to name some of them; the Swan in Akeman Street was my nearest and one which on special occasions we often visited, but there was also the Dolphin, Rose and Crown (a bit posh), the George, Robin Hood, Castle, Green Man, Anchor, Bell and another which I couldn't recall. Basil could only name three and Frank managed four, both claiming there were many more, so I think I won!

We did find in one shop something aimed at visiting troops. Some really lovely silk embroidered postcards. Mostly with a patriotic theme or 'missing you' message embroidered on the front, there was a space on the back for a message to a loved one. So I bought one for Florrie there and then. I had a sharp pencil with me so I purchased a stamp, wrote a brief message to Florrie and the children on the back and posted it! We're all assuming at some stage during its journey back to Blighty it will be intercepted by the census people and checked before going over to good old England.

Sunday arrived so we all decided to attend a church service held by our battery vicar. It was strange that with war all around us and young men being killed that the vicar spoke of peace and forgiveness for our fellow man. Being a practicing Christian I could understand what he meant, but looking at the faces of other soldiers, and airmen, in the congregation I could see puzzled looks on their faces, they were possibly thinking why forgive the Germans for the death and destruction they have caused. I did wonder if the Germans were holding similar services and praying for us!

We had a very pleasant surprise today which I must tell Florrie and the children about when we get some home leave. Straight from the front line, still in their dirty and muddy uniforms, we were entertained by a group of players calling themselves Billy Mack and the Optimists. They sang a little ditty called 'Cabbages, Ca-beans and Carrots'. They were really good and lifted our spirits no end. I pray they survive this terrible war when they go back to the front.

Talking of entertainment, one thing we all miss is a visit to one of our local picture houses to watch a good comedy film. Our nearest, like our local pub was at the other end of Akeman Street, and again not too far from our cottage, the Empire Picture Theatre, sometimes called the Gaiety. But we had another in competition with the Empire, the Gem cinema situated in the lower High Street. Tring might only be a small market town, but it wasn't short of entertainment!

The Battle of Delville Wood from 14 July to 15 September marked the start of the Second Phase of the Battle of the Somme. The attack did secure the British right flank, but at a cost in lives. Over 2,500 casualties in just five days from the South African 1st Infantry Brigade alone who held the wood from 15 to 20 July, its first foray into battle. Just one of many brigades deployed during this battle.

As for that King's Regulation. It was indeed mandatory that all ranks wore a moustache! KR 1695 from 1860 read - "The hair of the head will be kept short. The chin and the under lip will be shaved, but not the upper lip…"

Any soldier who shaved his moustache off faced severe disciplinary action by his commanding officer, which included military imprisonment. This fashion for hair over the upper lip was really a statement about virility and aggression. Beards and moustaches were particularly encouraged in places like India where bare faces were considered as not at all 'manly'. British soldiers posted there quickly found out that bare faces resulted in a great lack of respect from the natives!

On October 6 of 1916, the regulation was removed from KR and troops were allowed to be clean-shaven, mainly because the regulation was getting ignored in the trenches of WWI, especially as moustaches could get in the way of a good gas mask seal around the mouth. The order to abolish the growing of a moustache was signed by General Sir Nevil Macready who personally hated moustaches and was glad to finally be able to shave his off!

20 September

Our period of rest is now well and truly over. Attacks on the German front line had continued during our inactivity. Several major offences had taken place, none of which we took part in. The Battles of Pozieres, Guillemont and Ginchy had all taken place. We had heard the guns firing away in the distance from our site at Longueval, but took no part in any action much to our disappointment, as we were all eager to get back into the thick of it.

We believe we are somewhere near to Flers or Courcelette, but well back from the front lines. That mysterious grapevine has told us that we are supporting our army, together with the French Army, in a third and final offensive to push the Germans back to Germany and break the deadlock here on the Western Front. We can only hope and pray that we are successful and this dreadful, wasteful war will at last be over. Too many lives, on both sides, have been lost. Dear God let it end soon!

Our bombardment of the German trenches, defensive positions, and concrete pillboxes started on time in the early hours of this morning. We must be wreaking havoc and destruction on the German front line, but somehow we seem to fail to eliminate his infantry particularly his deadly machine gun positions, which we are told, are causing so many casualties among our advancing troops. The German dugouts must be very strong and deep down where our shells can't reach them.

We were told by our NCOs that for the first time those mighty tanks were used in action. They must have had a frightening, nightmarish effect on the moral of the defenders. To see these huge iron beasts slowly advancing, firing machine guns and artillery at pillboxes and defenders, would, I truly believe, make the most bravest of men turn around and run to the rear. We are all so glad that we are relatively safe being situated behind the lines, not having to face the machine gun, rifle fire, and shells of a determined enemy. So far we have not encountered any aggressive action by German artillery on our positions, but I have no doubt it will happen at some time.

As well as tanks we've heard, again by the grapevine, that a giant flamethrower was used against German troops for the first time. We've heard of flamethrowers being used on individual units of German troops, but this weapon sounds to be of huge construction.

This was the commencement of the third and final stage of the Battle of the Somme, this particular action lasting for one week. The tactical gains were far greater than expected, advancing the front line by up to 3,500 yards (3,200 meters), but the hoped for breakthrough to pass through the German lines was not achieved. The German infantry lost huge numbers of men.

For the first time Canadian and New Zealand troops were put into combat, as well as the newly formed Heavy Branch of the

Machine Gun Corp using tanks.130 tanks were first used in action on 15 September near the villages of Flers and Courcelette on the Somme. Not the success that had been hoped for mainly because these early tanks were prone to mechanical failure, they could be easily 'knocked out' by German artillery fire, and even small arms fire (they were very slow and therefore easy targets), plus the ground they were expected to operate upon was very boggy and churned up by shelling. In effect these tanks, and their crews, were being tested to ascertain if this new weapon was of any practical use in mechanised warfare.

The flamethrower was named the Livens Large Gallery Flame Projector, a truly massive flamethrower that was easily capable of burning everything up to 130 feet (40 meters). They were deployed for the first time at the Battle of the Somme by the British Army, and were quite effective.

Named after its inventor William Howard Livens, an engineering officer in the Royal Engineers. Only four of these experimental flamethrowers were deployed in offensives during the war. Two were destroyed at the Battle of the Somme before they could be used in 1916; the other two were used near Diksmuide no doubt terrifying the German defenders.

From February 1916 the 183rd Tunnelling Company of the British Army dug four saps (tunnels) that held a single Livens Large Gallery Flame Projector. However two of these saps were destroyed by German artillery fire, the two remaining were used to great effect at Carnoy. Reports from the time claim that German soldiers surrendered immediately after this truly terrifying weapon was fired.

This weapon was of huge proportions, being some 56 feet (17 meters) long and weighing some 2.5 tons. It took over 300 men to transport and assemble it in the saps. Although a truly terrifying weapon it could only hold enough inflammable liquid for three bursts of fire.

End of September.

We all seem to have lost all sense of time and days of the month! Basil and Frank are not too sure of the date. Basil reckons it's the 25th while Frank has opted for the 17th! Even our NCOs are not too sure! We have been kept so active moving up and down the line supporting our infantry that we're not entirely even sure where we are. We just get ordered to lumber up and move to a new position. It seems at times we have travelled miles, but we probably haven't. The roads are so bad - what there is of them - that it does seem to take forever to get to our new gun positions. Hauling heavy guns out of shell holes filled with mud and filthy water will take its toll on the fittest of men. Although we are fed quite well and fairly regularly it takes an enormous amount of physical energy moving guns and equipment.

I feel sorry for the horses that have to pull our heavy guns along. They must be suffering quite badly, although they do get well looked after by their handlers and are rested, fed and watered at the end of the day. The big difference between these lovely creatures and us is they have no idea why they are here enduring the same risks of death and injury as their human companions. They really have no choice in the matter. I hate to see these magnificent animals being used like this. We very often see dead horses killed by shellfire lying alongside the tracks, very sad.

Frank, Basil and the rest of the boys all have the appearance of much older men, unshaven faces, dirty and muddy uniforms, and all looking very tired by the constant movements and being in action. How much longer will the offensive last for we all ask?

6 October

We were rested for a few days to enable us to get cleaned up and prepare new positions for the battery. I think we're somewhere near to a village or town called Le Sars or Le Transoy, at least that's what our NCOs tell us.

There has been heavy fighting up at the front although we weren't involved in it. We have ample ammunition but we have been told that more is being brought up to us to support an offensive on the Transloy Ridges held by the Germans.

Luckily for us the weather has been good with warm days and bright sunshine, but it looks as if that is all going to change shortly as black rain clouds are gathering above us. Not good news for our infantry in their trenches waiting for orders to attack. No-mans-land must be full of shell holes that, if it does rain, will quickly fill up turning the earth into heavy mud, hampering their advance.

8 October

The planned bombardment of the German lines was delayed today. We're not really surprised by this as the rain has arrived and it's coming down like stair rods! We've been ordered to stand down until the offensive gets underway.

13 October

Action at last. This comes as a relief after trying to keep ourselves and our equipment dry and up to scratch over the last few days. What the lads in the trenches must be going through doesn't bear thinking about. Unless they have good, sheltered dugouts they must be wet through.

We have huge piles of shells so we are expecting to be firing for several days although not continuously as our howitzers are often given new trajectories to hit targets picked out by forward observers and our spotter aircraft. Can you imagine that? Flying over the German lines spotting for our big guns with all of our shells flying through the air where the RFC (Royal Flying Corp) pilots are flying! Not for the faint hearted!

18 October

We are ordered to cease fire, praying our guns having obliterated the German lines to make the infantry attack successful and with the minimum of casualties. To hear our big guns fall quiet is a huge relief, the sudden hush can be described as deafening! The thunderous noise we create would terrify most young men, but like everything here, we just get used to it. War is truly a terrible thing.

The Battle of the Transloy Ridges lasted until 11 November. Bad weather throughout October and November caused delays to the British Third and Fourth Armies, and the French Sixth Army. The full scope of the offensive was reduced, the battle ending on 18 November. The Battle of Ancre from 13 to 18 November is acknowledged as being the final battle. After this, due solely by atrocious weather, heavy rain, snow and fog, waterlogged trenches and liquid mud filled shell holes, both sides ceased offensive operations. Larger operations resumed again during January the following year.

The Third Phase of the Battle of the Somme ended on 18 November after the Canadian 4th Division captured the German Regina Trench and also captured the Desire Support Trench on that day. Atrocious weather effectively stopped the offensive. Shell craters were filled with what is best described as liquid mud. Any soldier falling or sliding into one of these had virtually no chance of either saving himself or being saved. Movement on the battleground was almost impossible by either side.

Total Allied casualties for the Somme battles were 623,907, of which 146,431 were killed or missing. United Kingdom and Commonwealth casualties were more than 419,654 of which 95,675 were killed or missing. The French Army had 204,253 casualties of which 50,756 were killed or missing. As for the German Army, they suffered a total of up to 600,000 casualties of which 164,055 were killed or missing with approximately 38,000 being captured as prisoners of war. This was the most costliest of battles during World War 1 in respect of casualties. A German officer commentated after the battle that "Somme. The whole history of the world cannot contain a more ghastly word".

Total casualties on the Western Front from July to December 1916 amounted to approximately 947,289 (British and French forces) and the German Army approximately 719,000. An approximate total of some 1,666,289 casualties.

8 December

A move to Bussy les Daours a few miles east of Amiens. No one seems to know the reason for this as after a few days we are moved back to our old positions. 'Ours not to reason why, ours but to do and die.' The words of Alfred Lord Tennyson come to mind!

1917

1 January

New Years Day and it seems very quiet at the front. No sound at all of any big guns firing, theirs or ours. As we go into a New Year we are all wondering how long this terrible war will go on for. We've heard of the terrible loss of life during the Somme offensive and we all do wonder how any nation can carry on after such huge losses of its young men. But we remain ever cheerful and optimistic that we will win and push the German invaders back to Germany.

All is not doom and gloom as Frank, Basil, myself and the rest of the battery crews all managed to stay awake to see the New Year in. Although we are behind our lines here at Le Transloy or Le Sars - we're still not sure exactly where we are - our celebrations were quiet. Our officers and NCOs managed to scrounge some fine rum for all the men and we all toasted the New Year in together, each man making his own wish and prayer for 1917.

We have some really first class officers and NCOs on our battery. Although the officers are very young for the most part - some look as if they should still be at school - as subalterns they do their best to get to know each man under their command, and although discipline and respect has to be maintained, they treat us as individuals and with respect - as we do them. This all helps to keep the battery working together and in fine fettle.

The NCOs, particularly the sergeants and above, are for the most part much older, many being part of the original BEF of 1914. We get our orders from them, and they get their orders through the chain of command from Battery Headquarters situated further behind us.

As it does seem quiet for the moment - the weather has put a stop to any fighting on both sides - we take the opportunity to clean ourselves up carrying out our routine of de-lousing our clothing and making our dugouts a bit more 'comfortable', so scrounging parties are sent out to find anything of any use to make our lives here a bit more civilised, something the boys at the front can't do. They rely on supplies being brought up to them on a daily basis from the rear. They and their trenches must be in a terrible state with all of this rain and even snow today. We count ourselves lucky that at least being back from the lines our dugouts and general living conditions are a lot better. We really all do feel sorry for the infantry.

I often think of Florrie and the children back home and wonder what they are doing now. We have family relations near to us where we live in Tring, so I suspect they will all be together at one cottage or another. I pray every day that they are all keeping well, I miss them so much especially young Robert who I left behind as a young baby. He will be just over a year old now, I do hope we get some leave to Blighty so that I can see them all again.

Messages from home arrive in dribs and drabs. They tend to follow us around France as we are moved from one position to another. It's amazing how they do find us eventually. I was hoping, as we all were, of a delivery from home while we are here, but as yet nothing has arrived.

Basil hasn't heard from his wife and family for a few weeks now, so is a bit down in the mouth. We try to keep his spirits up as best we can, but only a card or letter will cheer him up to his usual quiet, happy self. As for Frank, well he keeps us all laughing with his stories from the railways. What a laugh he is!

28 January

Things must be afoot. We were ordered to prepare for a rolling bombardment on a German strong point at Butte de Warlencourt to support the 8/10 Gordon Highlanders as they make a raid on this heavily fortified German position.

As it's classed as a raid we will have to cover the Highlanders withdrawal from the German position, so precision firing is called for, but we had been instructed in how to do this earlier by a practice raid demonstrated behind our positions by the 1st Australian Division, so we are confident that our guns and crews are up to the job.

The raiding party are to be dressed in white smocks and white painted helmets to help them blend into the snow lying on the ground, moving into no-man's- land by following black tape which had been positioned by engineers earlier. Rather them than me!

29/30 January

We started our shelling at 01.30 prompt to give covering fire to the raiding party. No doubt we will hear how the raid went later this week. As far as we're concerned our firing was accurate and we managed to achieve the desired effect of a rolling barrage ahead of the Scottish troops to keep the Germans under cover in their dugouts at the butte.

The German artillery fired on our positions this morning probably in retaliation of our raid earlier on. Their fire was pretty accurate and we unfortunately had 22 wounded who were caught out in the open by the ferocious shelling. Several of our guns were destroyed and others damaged, some beyond repair. Our dugouts were also damaged, some totally collapsing, but luckily the gunners trapped inside were quickly rescued unhurt. Not a good day for the 101st Siege Battery. Our first casualties of the war!

14 February

Valentines Day. Florrie and myself have always sent each other cards on this day, but with everything that's been happening I haven't been able to send her one, the first time I've missed. I hope she understands.

It's been a very busy and hectic few weeks. The guns, which were destroyed by German shelling, have been replaced and the damaged guns taken away to a maintenance unit for repair well back from the front. We've also received some new gunners to take the place of some of ours who were wounded and are still in a base hospital, so we are up to full strength again. It won't be too long before the new boys get into the swing of things. They all seem decent enough chaps. The dugouts have also been repaired, as have the gun pits and other positions.

We've also heard the results of the raid. It was a success with several German prisoners being taken for interrogation. Just 17 Scottish casualties against over 100 German casualties.

> Little opposition was met from the German defenders apart from three machine guns posts that were quickly attacked and eliminated. The main Scottish force attacked the butte and quarry while other parties advanced beyond the butte.
>
> At the butte some Germans refused to surrender so mortar bombs and Mills bombs (hand grenades) were thrown into the tunnel entrances starting several fires within the tunnels. Withdrawing after 25 minutes the raiding party returned to the British lines.
>
> Interrogation of the prisoners revealed that the butte was defended by 150 men, so there could have been up to 138 Germans trapped in the tunnels. At 03.15 there was a large explosion from the butte with flames reaching high into the sky above the mound, probably the result of hand grenades and other ammunition exploding in the tunnels.
>
> On 24 February the Australian 2nd Division occupied the Butte de Warlencourt after the Germans abandoned it in preparation for their own offensive, Operation Alberich, falling back to the well-prepared Hindenburg Line.
>
> Over the course of the war the Butte de Warlencourt changed hands more than once. On 24 March 1918 it was recaptured by the German 2nd Army when the Allies were forced to retreat during the

German offensive, Operation Michael. The butte was recaptured
for the last time on 26 August during the Second Battle of Bapaume

21 February

Today we moved to Corbie to the east of Bussy les Daours where we were for just a few days in early December. Arriving there in the early hours we were quickly ordered to move on to a position near to Albert, a place called Bellevue Farm. We all wondered if the top brass know what they are doing at times. This is the second time we have had a rapid move from Bussy les Daours. The move towards Albert is taking us back towards the Somme and the terrible battles of last year.

We are certainly on the move! The battery has now been ordered to move north towards Talmas then onto Bouquemaison with a possible further move north. We are all a bit 'lost' now, uncertain as to where we will eventually be positioned. Frustration at not being in action is rising, but we keep telling ourselves 'patience'!

23 February

We think all of our movements were to reorganise the RHA and RGA, as we are now part of the 13th Company, RHA and RGA under a Colonel Capp.

While getting ourselves reorganised and getting to know our new officers and NCOs we have received a delivery of letters and cards from home which it seems, have been chasing after us during our recent 'unsettled' moves from one place to another. Welcome news indeed!

We all received at least two letters. Florrie wrote to say that she and the children were keeping well although Robert has been unwell with a chill which turned into a nasty cold and cough, but he is a lot better now. As for Lillian she is now approaching four years of age and very soon will be off to Gravely School in Tring, a school for infants. It's a lovely school with some really good teachers, I'm sure she will settle into it. Florrie made no mention of receiving any of my cards to her which is surprising. Perhaps for some reason they are taking longer to get through our census people.

I do miss them all terribly. There is no mention of home leave for us gunners as yet, although some officers are allowed leave back to Blighty if they can be spared.

Two of our wounded from the earlier German shelling on our positions have been repatriated back to a hospital in Kent. Both sadly had legs amputated, suffering appalling injuries, so for them the war is well and truly over. We all wish them the very best. I do hope that that is not the only way we will get back home which seems so many miles away from us all in France.

Frank and Basil are a lot happier now that they have at last received news from their families. The three of us seem to stick together and generally do things together. We heard earlier that some leave to the rear might be on offer to the longer serving gunners, that includes the three of us, so here's hoping! Others have told us that there are a few decent towns around abouts where we can get some rest and look around the various shops and have a beer or two. None of us are really keen on this French lager stuff, it's too gassy and pretty tasteless, as well as being over priced! If we do get some time in the rear it will only be for a couple of days, but a nice break away from the dugouts and army rations! I'll look out for one or two of those silk postcards that the French make and sell to send to Florrie.

We usually pay a visit to one of the TocH establishments where you can get a really good meal for a small charge and kip down for the night. We need to thank the Reverend 'Tubby' Clayton for providing these very welcome houses which are open to all ranks as an alternative to the 'other recreational' life of most front line towns! They're run on Christian principals which is fine for me being a Christian, something that is difficult to be at the front with services few and far between. Basil and Frank always join me in prayer when we stay there, although they are both not too religious.

Neville Talbot, a senior British Army chaplain within the Church of England recruited other chaplains to serve on the Western Front. One of these recruits was a certain Reverend Phillip Byard Clayton who was 'posted' to the East Kent and Bedfordshire Regiments. Sent to France in 1915 he was then sent to Poperinge in Belgium, a short distance from Ypres.

Poperinge, or 'Pops' as British troops called it, was a very busy transfer station where troops were billeted en-route to and from the Flanders battlefields. The Reverend Clayton became affectionately known as 'Tubby' Clayton, and was instructed by Neville Talbot to organise a rest house for the soldiers. He selected an empty property abandoned by its owners, paying to these owners a rent of 150 FF each month. In need of repair caused by German artillery fire, British Royal Engineers set about this task and on 11 December 1915 it opened its doors.

'Tubby' Clayton decided immediately not to follow the lines of traditional church clubs and meeting houses and set up what he called an Everyman's House naming his establishment Talbot House in honour of Neville Talbot's brother, Lieutenant Gilbert Talbot, who had been killed in action previously in the year.

Soldiers being soldiers soon abbreviated the name to the initials 'TH', this in turn became TocH, the radio operators phonetic alphabet of the day as Toc Aitch. Religious services were taken in a chapel in the attic known as the 'Upper Room'. After the war ended in 1918 the interior was transported to London and displayed in the crypt of All Hallows-by-the-Tower. This organisation is still in existence today, the author is a member of this very worthwhile organisation.

13 March

We are now at a small town called Thelus, in fact we are at the mill. Early this morning we received an SOS call, we think from Canadian troops, who were in need of a concentrated, heavy bombardment on German positions about three miles away at Vimy Ridge. We can only assume that the Germans were attacking the Canadian lines there. This is the first time we have been called upon to support troops from Canada. We all hope our shelling was of some help to them.

15 March

This evening we received orders to move to Maroevil a few miles to the south west of our present position. This was accomplished with some difficulty as the road network here is not very good, either non-existent or damaged by shelling and flooded shell holes. I'm glad the officers know which way to go, for we are all completely dis-orientated with these sudden moves. We are all hoping that when we arrive we will be positioned at existing gun pits and have the chance to get cleaned up and carry out some much needed maintenance on our guns. How the army knows what to send, and where and when is above the heads of all of us, the organisation to keep us stocked with shells, food and water must be huge!

We were informed tonight that we would be staying here for a while, hooray! The largest town to us is Arras, a mile or so to the south. Perhaps we might get some time off to visit? That would be good. To get a break if only for a few hours would be welcome.

1 April

We have been so busy this is the first time I've really had to bring my diary up to date. We are now well stocked with shells so something big is going to happen. Rumours are that we are going to support the Canadians again at Vimy Ridge where they face the German trenches. This could be part of an offensive to dislodge the Germans from the ridge that gives them a tremendous advantage over us as they can see for miles around and are able to watch our every move.

4 April

The rumours were correct! We gave a really heavy and constant bombardment against the German trenches and fortifications at Vimy Ridge. Our co-ordinates were centered on Hill 145, a vital point to be captured by the Canadians. We all hope and pray our shelling was of great help to them in achieving success.

The weather has been really terrible with severe frosts, heavy rain and even snowstorms, not the best weather to start an offensive. Good luck to the Canadian troops, may God be with them.

10 April

Another move after our shelling of Vimy, this time to La Coulotte near Lens.

1 May

We are now attached to the 1st and 2nd Divisions of the Canadian Corp, an honour indeed we felt, to be fighting alongside our Dominion comrades from far-flung Canada.

The offensive that we have been taking part in is known to us as the Battle of Arras. It's not unusual to be in the dark about targets and objectives until the fighting is virtually over, although we all believe there is more to come as we are still being kept busy shelling German lines and more shells are being supplied to us by the service troops behind our positions.

6 May

Moved to CBSO (Counter Battery Staff Officer) at a Canadian Camp possibly somewhere near to Fresnov. We had a bit of an artillery duel with some German gun positions, unfortunately six of our lads were wounded in the exchange and were taken to the rear for treatment, probably going to an ADS (Advanced Dressing Station). We all hope their injuries are not too bad and they will be back with us as soon as they are fit. I do feel sometimes our lads are sent back to the front far too early after being wounded.

An ADS, or Advanced Dressing Station was the first 'port of call' for wounded troops after receiving immediate, possibly life saving, attention on the battlefield.

I know of one that still exists to this day, the British Army Advanced Dressing Station, Essex Farm, on the Ypres Salient. This

*Aid Station together with its bunkers was restored and preserved in
the early 1990s.*

*Originally established as rough dugouts during the Second Battle
of Ypres (1915) to provide basic medical treatment to wounded British
Army soldiers on the banks of the Ypres -Yser canal at the rear of what
is now the Essex Farm Military Cemetery.*

*These very basic dugouts were extended and heavily reinforced
with concrete to develop into a series of treatment rooms and much
larger medical treatment centre to manage the large numbers of
casualties being evacuated there. Many an Allied soldier passed
through this, and other ADSs before being sent further to the rear of
the front lines for hospitalisation.*

14 May

On the move again, this time back to La Coulotte where we traced our
steps and moved back into our old gun positions that required some
attention. There is so much happening and so fast that there's hardly
time for me to keep my diary up to date.

16 May

Apart for some supporting fire towards the German lines over the last
few days, all now seems very quiet, perhaps at last the offensive, and
even the war, has come to an end?

Our six walking wounded returned to us yesterday. Luckily they all
received superficial wounds which were treated easily and quickly at the
ADS. It would appear that they were very fortunate not to have suffered
worse injuries as the shell that nearly got them exploded into the soft
earth and mud preventing the deadly shrapnel from flying through the
air. We all think they have used up eight of their nine lives in one go!

*The Battle of Arras lasted from Easter Monday on 9 April until 16
May 1917 with the attack on Vimy Ridge being a wholly Canadian
Corp offensive. The ridge had been held by the German Army since
late 1914. The French Army held this part of the Western Front*

and attempted to occupy the ridge in May and September of 1915 but failed. During early 1916 this sector was taken over by the British Army from the French. The offensive was a Canadian Corp operation and is often referred to by Canadians as a coming of age, the time that Canada became a truly independent nation within the British Empire.

The attack was well planned. Tunnels dug towards the German lines meant that the Canadian troops could advance under no-mans-land in safety and without detection by the defending German 6th Army. The Royal Flying Corp played an important role gaining air superiority over the line. April was known as 'Bloody April' by the RFC because of the considerable cost in aircraft and pilots lost.

The RFC commenced its operation earlier, on 4 April, the same day and time that British artillery units shelled the German trenches. RFC losses were some 75 aircraft shot down and 105 pilots becoming casualties of which 19 were killed, 13 wounded and 73 reported as missing.

The weather on the day of the Canadian attack was very poor with snow and heavy rain intermixed. Starting at 05.30 the Canadians advanced finally taking the German trenches after fierce fighting on the night of 12 April. The Canadian Corp was now in full control of the ridge, but at a cost of 10,602 casualties of which 3,598 were killed and 7,004 wounded. German losses are not known, but it has been estimated that some 4,000 German defenders were taken as prisoners of war. The Allies now had a commanding view of the countryside stretched out before them.

2 June

We moved back to our earlier position at Thelus today having been told by our NCOs that we will be staying here for the rest of June at least. Hooray! We don't mind these moves to old gun emplacements as, apart from some improvements and repair work to them, we don't thankfully, have to start from scratch preparing gun pits and our own dug outs in case of German shelling.

4 June

We're now well settled in. We've made improvements to our dugouts, many with wooden floors and bunk beds which we made from old trench revetments, very nice, a decent place to eat and sleep at long last! As for eating, doesn't the Army know that there is only so much tinned bully beef the British soldier can eat! How many different ways can it be prepared? Sliced in some very good bread, or fried and put into a sandwich!

Our post caught up with us today! We all had several cards from home telling us the latest news on the home front. I myself had three cards from Florrie and a couple from friends back in good old Tring. I've almost forgotten what my hometown looks like as so many thinks have happened to me since I've been away, things I'd much rather forget about. I can't wait to get some leave, but I fear that is going to be very unlikely unless I get a 'Blighty wound' and am sent home to recover.

Florrie and the children are all well and coping with the food rationing which is in place thanks to those blasted horrible German U-Boats that sink merchant shipping bringing supplies to Britain. Florrie doesn't say how much rationing there is, so I suspect that those back home aren't allowed to say to keep our moral up here at the front.

One good thing in living in the countryside is that Florrie should have good access to local produce, milk, bread, butter, eggs, cheese and the like. We know one of the local dairy owners very well, a Mr. Pitkin, who has a good-sized dairy herd and a shop in Tring High Street next to the fire station where he sells his produce. I really do worry a lot about Florrie and the children, and everybody I know back home and pray every night that they are safe and sound.

The children are in good health and Lillian is doing well at school. We're lucky where we live as a few hundred yards away from our little cottage is Tring Park and Tring Mansion, the home of the Rothschild family. Walter Rothschild has zebras and emus roaming freely in the private part of the park and has constructed a natural history museum just a few doors away from our cottage with free entry to the museum for anybody. I really do miss my home! Most of all though I miss little

Robert. I wonder how he is growing up? He should be starting infants'
school in a year or so, I hope he'll be alright, but I'm sure Lillian will
take good care of him as she is already there.

Well, duty calls now. I'm on look out duty tonight at the battery
communication dugout in case Fritz starts anything. My job is to sound
the alarm and get all the gun crews mustered and ready for orders to
respond to anything Fritz might try.

9 June

Today a 'ceasefire' was declared on both sides. At long last both sides
have the opportunity to bury their dead.

We were transported by army truck to the front line, leaving just a
few gunners at their posts 'just in case!' What met us at the front line
and no-man's-land cannot be described by any words in the English
language. Across no-mans-land were the rotting bodies, and parts of
bodies, of hundreds, if not thousands, of soldiers, British and German.
Our task was to recover our dead for proper burial and where we can,
remove their identity discs so that their resting place can be recorded
and identified, sadly though many of these discs are missing so we bury
them as an unknown soldier, but in many cases we have to place more
than one into a mass grave. I will not describe in this diary what horrors
we witnessed.

British and German troops walking together in no-mans- land
recovering bodies was a really strange and eerie sight. We didn't attempt
to talk to them and they made no effort to join us in conversation. We
were ordered in no uncertain terms to do our duty and not to engage
the enemy in conversation, for that is what they still are, our enemy.
We were not to even exchange cigarettes or anything else with them as
happened at Christmas 1914.

For three days we did this. Something I would never wish to see
or do ever again. War is criminal and utterly senseless, it doesn't prove
anything, except who can slaughter more young men than any one
else! To find, remove and bury the remains of so many young men was
heartbreaking, but we did it. Frank and Basil, like myself, just got on

with the job. After a while the tears stopped running down our faces, we became immune and hardened to it all. If we weren't all strong willed and able to close our minds to this grim task I think we would have all gone crazy. Some of the lads had to be taken off this grim duty, they just couldn't cope with it.

Officers and NCOs would record each dead man's name and serial number into a logbook, if his name was known, for later reference and for that telegram which would be sent to relatives saying that this soldier was no longer listed as missing in action, but had been killed in action. What a grim task.

Writing this is such a struggle for me. I can still see those wretched bodies as we placed them with great respect into hessian sacks, no way for brave lads to end up. I'm finishing now, enough is enough. I have made myself a solemn promise never to tell another living soul what we all witnessed over the last three days, and indeed what has happened during our time over here. I pray to God that this war ends soon. Why do nations solve their differences by slaughtering their young men!

1 - 5 July

Some rapid moves over the last four days. First to Bruay then Haverskeque and Eeck finally arriving at Ypres today, the 5th. I'm sure I've spelt some, if not all, of these names wrong. We don't get written instructions, just verbal and sometimes it's difficult to remember exactly where we are going, such is war.

The battery is now attached to the XIX Company of the Royal Horse Artillery commanded by Brigadier General Pritchard DSO. Something big must be afoot. The Germans have apparently been sending out patrols to capture British troops to get information from them, plus there are constant patrols by German aircraft over our lines and even to the rear where we are positioned.

If something is going to break we hope it doesn't start too soon as our guns are in need of some specialised maintenance at our rear workshops. We can carry out routine servicing but the heavy machinery to strip our guns down is a specialised job, one which we cannot do.

8 July

It seems we are going to be here for sometime so we make ourselves as comfortable as we can, improving the dugouts and reinforcing our gun pits with extra sand bags and improved camouflage. Those German spotter aircraft are making a real nuisance of themselves, flying over our positions most days, and often more than once. Our lads in the RFC manage to get up and take them on, but if the German pilots spot them they are off like a shot back to their own lines with any photographs they have taken of our trenches and our gun emplacements. We are all sure that the Germans are planning a big offensive on our lines, but when it will be no one seems to know.

10 July

Our guns were taken to our rear workshops this morning for some well deserved maintenance. Let's hope Fritz didn't spot the move as we are now well under gunned at the battery.

August

I'm in one of our hospitals, No 11 Station Hospital, well to the rear of the lines along with most of the gunners in our battery including Frank and Basil. Fritz must have spotted our move to the workshops as shortly after the guns had gone he shelled us very heavily with gas shells.

As far as I can make out all but two of our battery are here with me, all suffering from the effects of gas. I'm not too bad, and Frank and Basil seem OK, but some of the lads are really suffering. I don't think they will all recover from this latest German means of conducting war! Although we were wearing gas masks our very bushy moustaches prevented the mask from getting a good seal around the face, so our moustaches are being shaved off before we go back, and we will tell any gunner we see sporting one to shave it off.

One of our officers, Captain R. T. Butler, paid us a visit which was well received by us all. It's nice to know that he cares about his men and has taken the time to get away from the battery to see how we are all getting along and give us the latest news.

He told us that by the middle of July we only had four guns operating which Captain Butler positioned to best effect to shell the Germans. A few days after this, Captain Butler thinks it was the 20th, the Germans again shelled what was left of our battery and destroyed three guns leaving just one still operating. It was during this attack that Gunners Bennet and Evens were both badly wounded from shrapnel. I don't know these two lads as they are replacements who only arrived with us a couple of days before they were both wounded. What a welcome to the battery!

Captain Butler was showing the strain of what had been happening. His hands were visibly shaking and he smoked constantly, one after the other. It must be really grim at the battery. Because of casualties the battery is one officer and 20 gunners under strength, most of these being affected by the gas and probably here in the same hospital.

He did have some encouraging news to tell us however. On the 31 July XIX Corp and 5 Command attacked along their front taking some 6,000 German prisoners together with over 100 German officers. Good news indeed. Giving the Boche a taste of their own medicine!

The three of us expect to be returned to duty very soon, although for some of the lads the war is well and truly over. I wouldn't want the task of informing their families of their deaths far, far from home.

3 September

Today we were returned to the front line. Having mostly recovered from the gas attack we were considered to be fit for duty. Some of us believed we were being returned too early as we were all coughing frequently from the lasting effects of breathing in gas. This early returning of soldiers to the front was something I had suspected for some time, now I knew I was correct.

We were now with the 31st Siege Battery. It's rumoured that our old unit, the 101st, is to reform behind the lines due solely to its losses in men and equipment. I'm not at all surprised if that's true as they took a real pasting from German guns.

We're still somewhere near to Ypres supporting the 5th Army in an attack on a place called Hessian Wood. It's been raining very heavily so our barrage was delayed by some three hours. The wood is heavily defended by German troops in dugouts and machine gun positions, so we all hoped our barrage was effective, although we don't envy our lads attacking in what must be terrible conditions following the heavy rain. God bless all of them.

5/6 September

Last night our battery was called upon to support an attack by the 125th Brigade at a place called Iberian and in particular Hill 35. We laid down a barrage of four rounds for one minute to each gun, but we, like other crews, fired 10.

15 September

The fighting must be very heavy. We've heard stories of attacks by our lads and counter attacks by the Germans resulting in tremendous casualties on both sides. Our attack last week to take Hill 35 failed, and we've been told that other attacks on the hill since have not been successful.

Our own battery casualties from German shelling must be causing a problem. It looks as if the 100th and 101st Siege Battery has been amalgamated into other batteries as we had an intake from both to replace our casualties today.

At Zanovoorde now supporting II Corp who are to attack a German Command Post.

The Battle of Passchendaele, officially known as the Third Battle of Ypres, lasted from 31 July to November 1917. The German Army had for some time wanted to capture Ypres, which apart from being the principle town in the area was also located within a salient, or bulge, jutting into territory held by the Germans. Several attempts were made to capture it; the First Battle of Ypres, October to November 1914; and the Second Battle of Ypres, April to May 1915.

Field Marshall Sir Douglas Haig decided that there would be a major British offensive in the Ypres sector. The British Second and

Fifth Army which attacked the German Fourth Army, was severely hampered by very heavy rainfall which, because of earlier heavy shelling, turned the battlefield into a muddy quagmire, hampering the British advance. The much expected quick break through into the German lines was never achieved and the battle turned into a continuous battle of attrition.

The German Army was well aware of an impending offensive, the ensuing British artillery bombardment on their positions was, in effect, a final warning to the defenders that an attack was about to take place. The shelling lasted for some two weeks, expending some 4.5 million shells from over 3,000 artillery pieces. But this vast bombardment failed to destroy the heavily fortified German strong points and positions.

31 July saw the infantry attack, but all of the shelling has destroyed the existing water drainage system and as a result the clay soil became a sticky quagmire. Although the left flank of the attack did manage to achieve its goals, the right flank completely failed.

The heaviest rainfall for over 30 years made any movement over the terrain practically impossible, turning the ground into thick liquid mud which prevented tanks from supporting the troops whose weapons were very often useless as mud made their rifles quite unserviceable. Both men and horses that slipped or fell into any of the thousands of shell holes that covered the battlefield would drown, to escape was virtually impossible even with the help of comrades. The offensive was halted until 16 August.

For another month neither side could make any effective attacks, but with an improvement in the weather during the middle of September the offensive was resumed on the 20th. The Battle of Menin Road Ridge; the Battle of Polygon Wood (26 September) and the Battle of Broodseinde (4 October) enabled the British Army to occupy the ridge to the east of Ypres.

Further attacks during October resulted in no appreciable progress being made. Passchendaele, or what remained of it, was captured by British and Canadian soldiers on 6 November. This gave Field Marshall Sir Douglas Haig a valid reason to call off the offensive, claiming it as a success. Passchendaele was just five miles from the offensive's starting point!

What had taken over three months to achieve had cost the Allies some 325,000 casualties (the British Army alone lost 244,897 men either killed, wounded or missing) and the German Army an estimated 260,000. It made little difference to the Ypres salient. A German General Staff officer did accept however that the German Army and therefore Germany had been brought to the brink of 'certain destruction' due to German losses in Flanders.

1918

It should be noted by the reader that no War Diaries or any other records after 17 September 1917 are known to exist for the 31st Siege Battery RGA. All were destroyed during the Battle of Passchendaele. So for us this is where my grandfather Reginald Robert Cato, Frank Chapman and B. C. Gribble's journey ends.

All that is known is that during a German gas attack on their positions somewhere close to Ypres all three, and possibly more, were killed in action at their battery on Sunday 10 March 1918, and were finally buried together in Ypres at the Ypres Reservoir Cemetery.

The gas attack was probably a prelude to the forthcoming German Spring Offensive or Kaiserschlacht (Kaiser's Battle) along the Western Front commencing 21 March, which was in effect the last German offensive in an attempt to break through the Allied lines. This offensive came to a halt on 18 July when the German Army literally 'ran out of steam'.

There were four main German offensives with the codenames of 'Michael', 'Gneisenau', 'Georgette' and 'Blucher-Yorck'. The German main attack was 'Michael', its intention was to break through the Allied front line and outflank British forces, and eventually after a rapid advance, to defeat the British Army forcing the French Government to seek an armistice. The other three offensives were hoped to divert Allied forces from the main German attack.

The initial German attacks were successful, driving the British Army back some miles at the cost of many casualties to both sides. In an effort to stem and halt the German advance the Allies withdrew to strategically important areas - the Channel ports and important railway junctions - giving up strategically worthless ground to the attacking Germans.

The reason for the German failure in the offensive was in fact its initial success. The advance by the German Army was so rapid, mainly thanks to a new German tactic of using lightly armed, but fast moving Storm Troopers, that they literally ran out of food and ammunition as the German supply lines were so far stretched that the supply troops could not keep pace with the rapid advance, so eventually all offensives came to a halt.

German troops who captured British supply dumps were amazed at the quality and quantity of supplies held in them. Food and drink of all description were there for the taking, which the German troops did. This was a big loss of moral for these troops as they had been told that the British Army was starving and on the point of total collapse, which of course, was total nonsense. It could be claimed that at this point in the war the German troops realised that for them, the war was lost.

By the end of the offensive the Germans had large territorial gains, but the overall victory for which they had planned was not achieved. Their army was exhausted and held poor defensive positions.

This was a turning point for the Allies. Troops from the United States of America were deployed for the first time as independent units. The initiative was now clearly with the Allies who very soon would begin what is referred to as the Hundred Days Offensive, which after four long and costly years would bring the war to end at 11.00 on the morning of 11 November 1918.

Epilogue

This is the end of the story, true in part, of three comrades in the RGA who served together and finally died together. All records from December 1916 to February 1917 for the 101st and 31st Siege Battery were destroyed by German shelling or flooding at the battery. War diaries from 15 September 1917 were all destroyed in battle, and as such no records exist to inform us as to what action or under what circumstances Gunners Reginald Robert Cato, Frank Chapman and B. C. Gribble were killed in action. We can be sure however that all three succumbed to a German gas attack on their battery near Ypres on 10 March 1918.

Their last resting place is in the Ypres Reservoir Cemetery where they are buried alongside each other, comrades together. It is our intention, that while we are able to, is to make an annual pilgrimage to place a small wooden cross on each grave as an act of respect and remembrance for the grandfather I never knew and his two friends.

Reginald Robert Cato never managed to get home to see his son Robert again. As far as I am aware no photographs of him are in existence. His medals together with the 'dead man's penny' plaque and certificate have long since vanished which is a great shame. In essence, apart from his last resting place, and now this book, there is no family record of my grandfather Reginald Robert Cato in existence anywhere.

It is very unlikely that Gunner B. C. Gribble ever managed to get home leave, and, like my grandfather, never saw his wife again.

My searches for any living relatives of Frank Chapman and B. C. Gribble have sadly so far resulted in none being located, but I do intend to continue researching in an effort to trace and inform any living relatives of the location of their forebears' graves.

We often attend the playing of the Last Post at the Menin Gate Memorial in Ypres where the names of over 54,000 soldiers are listed who died before 16 August 1917, and have no known grave. This is an occasion for me to wear the duplicate medals that were awarded to my grandfather as a sign of respect to the grandfather I never knew.

My mother would never allow poppies (which grew profusely in local meadows) to be brought into our small cottage in Akeman Street, Tring, which for many years as a young boy puzzled me. The answer however, became clear later on in my life. The poppy has become the national symbol of mourning and remembrance at the annual Act of Remembrance at the Cenotaph in Whitehall, stemming from the poppies that grew on the battlefields of the First World War. The poppies obviously reminded her of her father whom she never really knew.

Wherever they lay, may they all Rest in Peace

Barry Woodhouse

Howitzer being prepared for action. 1917.
Archive photograph. Copyright not known.

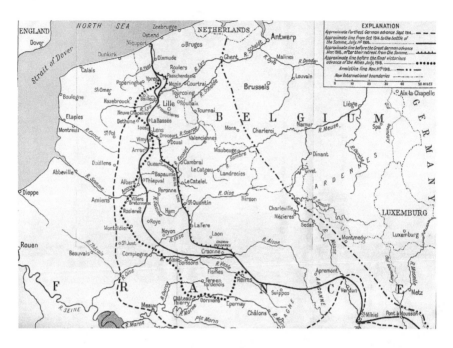

The Western Front 1914 – 1918. – Author's collection.

Our old cottage in Akeman Street, Tring at the end of the 19th century is directly below the tall chimney stack on the left. This is where Reginald Robert Cato was born. By coincidence the author was also born here in 1941. Full circle indeed! – Author's collection.

Looking from the other direction. Our cottage is the second door on the right from the archway. Just where the road bends by the tall chimney stack. – Author's collection.

Photographed further along Akeman Street. The tall chimney stack is just visible at the bottom right. – Author's collection.

Wallabies or kangaroos roaming freely in Tring Park in the early 20ᵗʰ century. The author's mother often spoke of seeing these as well as zebras in the Rothschild area of the park. The Rothschild mansion is in the background. – Author's collection.

*Ostriches in Tring Park.
Author's collection.*

A crew training on a 6 inch howitzer at Lydd Training Camp.
Author's collection.

TRACTOR WITH SIEGE HOWITZER

Pulling a siege howitzer by tractor.
Author's collection.

Howitzers of a siege battery, Royal Garrison Artillery, firing from the Fricourt-Mametz Valley in August 1916. Battle of the Somme. – Author's collection.

Gunners of the 95th Siege Battery loading a 9.2 inch howitzer near Bayencourt during the Battle of the Somme 1916. – Author's collection.

British artillery dugouts near Ypres 1918.
Author's collection.

A knocked out British tank. The Ypres salient 1919.
Author's collection.

Heavily shelled trenches at the Ypres salient 1919.
Author's collection.

Ypres Cloth Hall as it was pre 1914. Author's collection.

The Cloth Hall as it was in 1919. Author's collection.

The Cloth Hall following restoration c1921.
Author's collection.

The Cloth Hall in 2018.
Copyright June Woodhouse.

A silk postcard of the type mentioned in the diary.
Author's collection.

The author and his wife at the graves of Gunners B. C. Gribble, Reginald Robert Cato and Frank Chapman on the occasion of commemorating their deaths 100 years to the day. 10 March 2018. Copyright the author.

Copyright the author.

Sources

My own knowledge of the First World War, and for confirmation of that knowledge I have consulted and referred to the following. At the time of publication all named web sites were correct.

'Tring. A Pictorial History'.
Barry Woodhouse. Phillimore Publishers.

'Tring Born and Bred'.
Fred Woodhouse. Monroe Publishing.

Commonwealth War Graves Commission

www.wikipedia.org
Battle of the Somme
Attacks on the Butte de Warlencourt
Battles of the Western Front 1914-1918
Western Front (World War 1)
The First Battle of Passchendaele (Third Battle of Ypres)
The Second Battle of Passchendaele (Third Battle of Ypres)
Spring Offensive (1918)
Field Punishment
Livens Large Gallery Flame Projectors

www.wwlbattlefields.co.uk
World War 1 Battlefields. Vimy Ridge Canadian Battle ground.

www.encyclopedia.1914-1918-online.net/article/ypres_battles_of
The 3rd Battle of Ypres

www.bbc.co.uk/history/worldwars/wwone/battle_passchendaele.shtml
Battle of Passchendaele

www.nrm.org.uk/~/media/files/nrm/pdf/research/railway-workers-wwl

www.greatwar.co.uk/ypres-salient/remains-bunkers-essex
Advanced Dressing Station. Essex Farm. Ypres Salient.

Billy Mack and the Optimists
BBC Television. BBC1. 'Who do you think you are?' Lee Mack.

'Deborah and the War of the Tanks'.
John A. Taylor. Pen & Sword Publishers

'Time Team Special'.
Channel 4 Television. 'The Somme's Secret Weapon'.

BV - #0023 - 190319 - C0 - 234/156/5 - PB - 9781912183845